The Clumsy Angel and the New King

Words by Norman C. Habel
Pictures by Jim Roberts

Concordia Publishing House

A PURPLE PUZZLE TREE BOOK

COPYRIGHT © 1972 CONCORDIA PUBLISHING HOUSE, ST. LOUIS, MISSOURI
CONCORDIA PUBLISHING HOUSE LTD., LONDON, E. C. 1
MANUFACTURED IN THE UNITED STATES OF AMERICA
ISBN 0-570-06526-7

Years and years went by,
but the new King didn't come
to solve the purple puzzle
and rule the world for God.

Then one quiet, shining night
in the golden living room of heaven,
where all the tall, red angels meet
after work on earth is done,
they started singing softly
and tapping with their feet.

If you had sat that shining night
among those tall, red angels,
you'd have seen them kick aside
their fancy flying shoes
to sing and dance like this:

Tippy toe, tippy toe, tinsel,
Glory to God in heaven.
Tippy toe, tippy toe, tinsel,
We spin around the earth.
Tippy toe, tippy toe, tinsel,
Glory to God in heaven.
Tippy toe, tippy toe, tinsel,
We watch each baby's birth.

Among those tall, red angels
was Gabriel the Great,
who always had his little horn
and simply couldn't wait
to blow it every morn.

Among those tall, red angels
was Michael with his sword.
He had to fight for God sometimes
because he was so strong.

Among those tall, red angels
one clumsy angel sat,
far away in a corner
curled up like a cat.
Shall we call him little Jack Horner?
What would you say to that?

Now that clumsy little angel,
who wasn't very shiny,
always stayed at home.
He had to clean the stables
of the horses in the sky
that angels rode across the earth,
very, very high.

Then God came into the living room
where all the angels sang.
And God was very bright.
He sat in a shining, purple chair
covered with candlelight.

Then one by one the angels fell
down upon their knees:
Plink! Plink! Plink!
Everyone was buzzing,
waiting for a message
to fly across the seas.

"This job," said God, "takes everyone!
You and you and you
and Jack, the clumsy angel, too!"

Can you imagine the wild surprise
of all those tall, red angels?
They knew quite well
whenever a baby was due,
God would send one angel;
or maybe even two
if one day twins are born.
And that can happen, too!
But why send clumsy Jack?

"Now listen, Michael," said God.
"You are the first to go.
 You have to meet a good man,
 a carpenter called Joseph,
 and say to him, 'Don't fear.
 The young girl whom you love
 will soon have a Baby
 sent from heaven above.'

"You may have to fight old Satan
 somewhere on the way,
 for he whispered to that good man
 to try and run away.

"Are you listening, Gabriel?
Your job is very special.
You have to tell that young girl,
whose name is gentle Mary,
'God Himself is giving you
a very special Baby.'

"Even clumsy Jack!
You must leave the sky
and learn to fly
down to the earth
to see the birth
of this special little Boy.

"You know the ways of animals,
and you've lived inside a stable.
You have the biggest job of all.
Are you ready, willing, and able?

"When Mary rides her tired donkey
to the little town of Bethlehem,
you must fly beside him
and never let him fall.
When they reach that town,
you must find a stable
and lead the donkey there.
Make sure the stable doesn't have
any wild beast.
Then make the stable ready
for a very special Guest."

Jack, the clumsy angel,
jumped and jumped for joy.
At last he had a chance
to watch the birth of a Boy
in a very small stable
instead of in a house
with many, many toys.

"And all the other angels,"
said God, who was laughing for joy,
"must fill the sky that night
and sing to all the countryside
to make the heavens bright."

At last the angels asked
the most important question of all:
"Who is this Baby going to be?
And why is He so special
that all of us must go to earth
instead of one or two or three?"

"This Boy," said God,
"is My very own Son.
I will mold My Boy
deep in His mother, Mary,
just as I molded Adam
from fresh red clay.

"My Son will rule the world for Me
as Adam had to do.
My Son will solve the purple puzzle,
which Adam couldn't do.
My Son will be the new King
that all the prophets promised
for waiting people everywhere.
Jack, will you open the door?"

So off the angels went
singing their Christmas song:

Tippy toe, tippy toe, tinsel,
Glory to God in heaven.
Tippy toe, tippy toe, tinsel,
Peace to men on earth.
Tippy toe, tippy toe, tinsel,
Glory to God in heaven.
Tippy toe, tippy toe, tinsel,
We'll watch o'er Jesus' birth.

And that's the way it happened
when Jesus Christ was born.
Well, isn't it?
Jack, the clumsy angel,
hid beneath the manger
to keep both Mary and Jesus
safe from any danger.
Right?

If you ever see Jack,
don't be afraid at all.
For he can tell you all about
King Jesus in His stall.
But maybe Jack has a different name.
Would that matter at all?

OTHER TITLES

SET I.
WHEN GOD WAS ALL ALONE 56-1200
WHEN THE FIRST MAN CAME 56-1201
IN THE ENCHANTED GARDEN 56-1202
WHEN THE PURPLE WATERS CAME AGAIN 56-1203
IN THE LAND OF THE GREAT WHITE CASTLE 56-1204
WHEN LAUGHING BOY WAS BORN 56-1205
SET I LP RECORD 79-2200
SET I GIFT BOX (6 BOOKS, 1 RECORD) 56-1206

SET II.
HOW TRICKY JACOB WAS TRICKED 56-1207
WHEN JACOB BURIED HIS TREASURE 56-1208
WHEN GOD TOLD US HIS NAME 56-1209
IS THAT GOD AT THE DOOR? 56-1210
IN THE MIDDLE OF A WILD CHASE 56-1211
THIS OLD MAN CALLED MOSES 56-1212
SET II LP RECORD 79-2201
SET II GIFT BOX (6 BOOKS, 1 RECORD) 56-1213

SET III.
THE TROUBLE WITH TICKLE THE TIGER 56-1218
AT THE BATTLE OF JERICHO! HO! HO! 56-1219
GOD IS NOT A JACK-IN-A-BOX 56-1220
A LITTLE BOY WHO HAD A LITTLE FLING 56-1221
THE KING WHO WAS A CLOWN 56-1222
SING A SONG OF SOLOMON 56-1223
SET III LP RECORD 79-2202
SET III GIFT BOX (6 BOOKS, 1 RECORD) 56-1224

SET IV.
ELIJAH AND THE BULL-GOD BAAL 56-1225
LONELY ELIJAH AND THE LITTLE PEOPLE 56-1226
WHEN ISAIAH SAW THE SIZZLING SERAPHIM 56-1227
A VOYAGE TO THE BOTTOM OF THE SEA 56-1228
WHEN JEREMIAH LEARNED A SECRET 56-1229
THE CLUMSY ANGEL AND THE NEW KING 56-1230
SET IV LP RECORD 79-2203
SET IV GIFT BOX (6 BOOKS, 1 RECORD) 56-1231

the PURPLE PUZZLE TREE